# FINANCIAL BALANCE

WWW.AUTHORBRIJONES.COM

Bri Jones

*I dedicate this book to my son, you by far are amazing in every way. Words can't express how happy and blessed I am to be your mother. You always find a way to bring more joy to my life. Always do your best, because the sky is not your limit. Love you forever.*

# ACKNOWLEDGMENT

First and foremost, I want to thank God for the vision and knowledge to write this book. I also want to thank the best son any mother could pray for. My son is my biggest supporter and he inspires me to do my best and never give up.

I'd like to thank my illustrate David Martinez for his continuous hard work and staying onboard to designing this additional book cover. Thank you to my family and friends for their continuous support. Lastly, I want to thank you, the readers, for your support in purchasing my book. Everyone's support is greatly appreciated.

# INTRODUCTION

The information in this book is based on personal and professional experience. The results will vary depending on the reader's dedication. While reading this book, you will be equipped with the necessary decision-making tools to achieve financial balance by utilizing three main strategies Creating Passive Income, Budget Management, and Executing Credit Stability.

# VISION AND GOALS

*W*here there is no vision, the people perish: but he that keepeth the law, happy is he. -Proverbs 29:18 (KJV) (A man without a vision will perish)

*And the Lord answered me, and said, Write the vision, and make it plain upon tables, that he may run that readeth it.* - Habakkuk 2:2 (KJV)

What is your vision?

Have you ever taken the time to meditate and really think about what you want to do or accomplish in your life?

Don't make the mistake of following the vision of what you think other individuals feel you should accomplish or what you should do with your life. Yes, individuals can motivate you to be stronger or a better person, but they can also deter you from your purpose.

It is vital to meditate and spend time with God and seek his guidance in making your vision your reality.

Your vision can encompass many aspects such as finance, health, family, house, career, vehicles, travels or peace. With respect to this book, we are going to focus on achieving financial balance. After meditating, create a vision board or list. A vision board is typically created by cutting out articles, pictures or words from magazines that speak to your vision, then pasting the cutouts on a large or small poster. The vision list can be created as a bullet point list that demonstrates your vision on colored paper of your choice. The vision board is more favorable because it gives you a visual reminder, which is tied to your visual emotion. Make sure to put your vision board or list on the refrigerator, mirror, desk at work, vehicle dashboard or anywhere you will see it several times daily. The purpose is to remind yourself of your vision so you can start subconsciously moving toward achieving your vision.

Goals are a desired outcome set by a person according to his or her vision. In order to achieve a set goal, a plan and commitment have to be implemented.

Setting goals is a major factor in staying motivated in life. It is essential when you set goals to put your list in a location that you will see every day. This will remind you of the importance of staying committed to your plan. When you set goals, you are making a mental and emotional decision to accomplish something that will benefit you or someone close to you. There are no limits or restrictions on setting goals. Goals can be identified as complex or as simple as a daily routine. Goals can be set as short term or long term. A short term goal is something you set to achieve within a year. A long term goal is anything that would take you in excess of a year.

When setting a goal, you want to identify the purpose and plan for achieving the goal. The following are a few steps you should take.

• Acknowledge the sacrifices you will have to face. That would be any adjustments in your routine that you need to prepare to remove for the greater cause of reaching your set goal.

• Identify why the goal is significant to you. How does it directly affect you or someone close to you?

• Recognize what problems you will encounter in achieving the goal and create a solution for it.

• Outline the benefits of achieving the goal. Will it improve your health, create financial security, or provide a comfortable retirement?

• Make sure you have a good support group such as family, friends or resources to remind you of why you want to achieve the set goal. Prepare for any possible obstacles that would discourage you from reaching your goal.

• Don't be afraid to regroup and start over if something does occur out of your control. The art of success is not measured by how many times you have to start over but it's how you finish.

• Make sure you have consistent reminders and tactics to keep you on track. This could be by creating a vision board or a list of your plan of attack to execute your goal. Make sure this list is visible daily without effort. Putting the list in your plain view daily is imperative. It will have a direct effect on your behavior, attitude, and the success of meeting your goal.

• Decide how you are going to measure your progress. Identify your milestones and time line to meet those milestones.

• Create a reward system to celebrate achieving your success. Celebrate each milestone you meet; then, ultimately, celebrate your success in achieving your goal. This is critical especially if it's a goal that you feel will be a struggle.

Lena and Azra have a short term goal to lose 10 pounds each in 30 days. The purpose is so Lena can fit into a designer dress she purchased and Azra in a tailored suit he wore years ago for their twenty year class reunion. They plan to eliminate fast food, junk food and workout twice a day, before and after work. This short term goal will give Lena and Azra instant gratification, because they will see the results quicker than if it was a long term goals. It's still significant to incorporate motivational factors to stay on task even with short term goals.

When considering long term goals, more motivation is needed because it will take longer to see the results of the commitment. Shena has a long term goal to save $40,000 in five years. The purpose is for a down payment on her first home. Shena's plan is to exercise no excess spending, make smart investments, pay off her current debt, and create more passive income.

Motivational factors for both short and long term goals could be a daily visual of the target goal, support group, final reward, or anything that keeps you on track.

When setting goals, remember not to overwhelm yourself with too many goals at one time. This could cause discouragement. Don't be afraid of failure! Remember you can always start your plan over or pick up where you left off. Failure is a learning lesson. Learn from your mistakes and implement a different strategy or approach.

## Be Specific and Truthful When Setting Your Goals

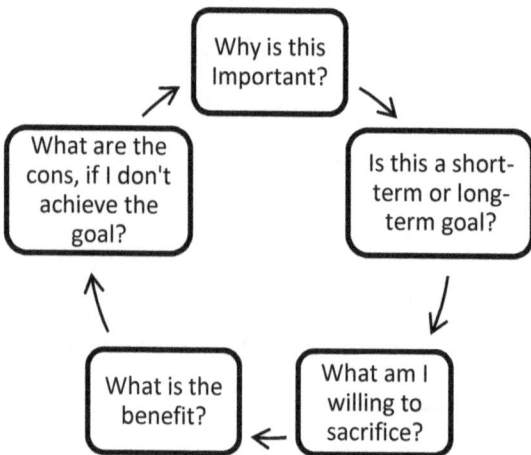

Why is this Important?

What are the cons, if I don't achieve the goal?

Is this a short-term or long-term goal?

What is the benefit?

What am I willing to sacrifice?

It is imperative for you to be truthful with yourself when setting goals. The more complex the goals, the harder it will be to reach them. Don't get discouraged by challenges. They will only make you stronger and wiser. If you take your goal plans seriously, you will successfully achieve your goal. However, you must be truthful, realistic, committed, and motivated. There will be times when you will feel discouraged, but if you have strong motivational factors in place use them to stay on course.

The process of setting goals will require you to mentally prepare yourself for the journey ahead. All goals require sacrifices no matter how long or short the journey. Identify the benefits of reaching your goal. Will it give you balance, peace, happiness, improve your health, create financial security, enable early retirement? Identify all the cons associated with not accomplishing your goal. Create a mindset that helps you realize not reaching your goal is not an option. **This is a Must!**

**Here are some financial goals to consider, be specific**

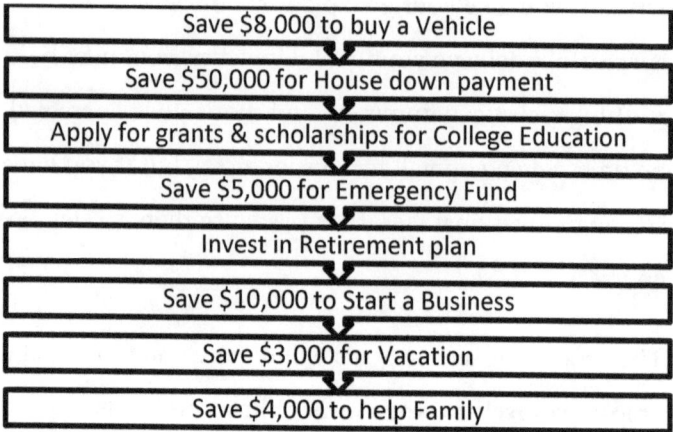

| Save $8,000 to buy a Vehicle |
| --- |
| Save $50,000 for House down payment |
| Apply for grants & scholarships for College Education |
| Save $5,000 for Emergency Fund |
| Invest in Retirement plan |
| Save $10,000 to Start a Business |
| Save $3,000 for Vacation |
| Save $4,000 to help Family |

**To achieve success in reaching your financial goals it is vital to:**

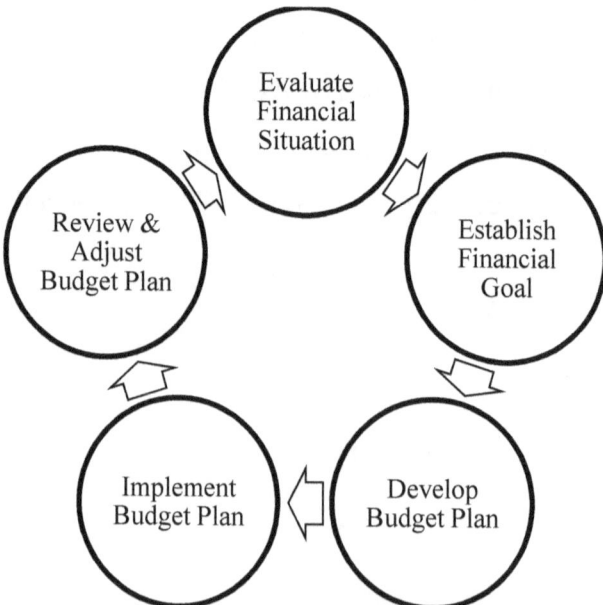

Evaluate Financial Situation

Establish Financial Goal

Review & Adjust Budget Plan

Implement Budget Plan

Develop Budget Plan

When developing your financial goal, you have to evaluate your current monthly financial circumstances. How much income do you bring home from any regular income source? What are your monthly expenses? Evaluate your accumulated expenses for one month. Collect all your receipts and take notes on anything and everything you spend money on. This will include mortgage/rent, utilities, groceries, eating out, gifts, entertainment, impulse shopping, anything and everything. You will be surprised, but this technique will give you awareness and a visual of your spending habits. Once you identify your total monthly income and total monthly expenses, then you can figure out your savings income which is sometimes referred to as disposable income. Savings/disposable income is money you have left after paying your taxes, expenses and other obligations.

**Monthly Income - Monthly Expenses = Disposable   Income**

Develop a financial goal that is realistic. You don't want to set a goal that is unachievable or set yourself up for failure. Evaluate your expenses and see what can be eliminated if your savings/disposable income is too low to achieve your goal. After you understand what your income and expenses are on an estimated monthly basis, this is when you create a budget plan. A budget plan can be designed in paper form or on an Excel spreadsheet. I recommend an Excel spreadsheet because once the formula is created you only have to enter your totals and Excel calculates everything for you. The budget plan is where you compare your estimated income/expenses versus your actual income/expenses. In addition, you create a limit (budget) of how much you will spend in specific areas of your expenses.

***Ready, Set, Go!*** Implementing your budget plan is actually putting your goal into action. When do you start and how are you going to start? Decide what is going to be your first step and stick to it! Every seven days you should be assessing your progress and making adjustments to your budget plan as needed. Don't make it too easy nor too stressful. You want to have a balance so you don't get overwhelmed or quit.

Remember: Quitting is Not an Option! After you get more comfortable with your budget plan, you should start monitoring your activities every 30 days. Budget Plan will be discussed in more detail in the upcoming chapters.

# GENERATE PASSIVE INCOME

*H onor the Lord with your wealth and with the best part of everything you produce. Then he will fill your barns with grain, and your vats will overflow with good wine.* - Proverbs 3:9-10 (NLT)

*The wise have wealth and luxury, but fools spend whatever they get.* - Proverbs 21:20 (NLT)

Passive income is commonly defined as earning money without being active or with little effort to maintain the flow of cash. Passive income can also be considered as doing something you were going to do anyway, but getting paid for it. Doing something you enjoy is not considered work. You're just getting paid for something you like to do. As most people can agree, they need more money but don't have enough time in the day or the energy to obtain another job. Some might not have the opportunity, experience, or background to accumulate the desired salary. However, everyone has a unique gift they can capitalize on. Sometimes the hardest part is discovering that talent. The mindset should be to create passive income that can be generated into recurring income after your initial efforts have been made.

If you look around your home, there is extra money laying there taking up space or in storage costing you more money. I am guilty of having a large storage unit for eight years and visiting the unit fewer than five times. I couldn't remember what exactly I had in the storage unit, but I was paying a monthly fee. My dad and brother asked my permission to save me money and clean out the unit. I gladly accepted. My dad and brother brought most of the items to my dad's basement so I could go through them. Out of the large storage unit, I decided to keep only three medium storage containers. The remaining items I donated to charity and daycare centers. I plan to sell the contents of the three storage containers online, at consignment stores, and at pawn shops. Even if you're not as bad as I, look around your home and see what you are collecting that you don't utilize, but someone else could. Sell your unused items to consignment stores, online, or pawn shops; or donate them to charity.

Manually balancing your checkbook, even if you bank

online, could save you money. Nothing human-made is without flaws. Most financial institutions use Information Technology (IT) systems to process transactions and fees on accounts. If you practice balancing your checkbook regularly, you could dispute bank errors, and avoid overdrafts and other unnecessary fees.

Take the time to research online survey companies that have a payout in your area. There are several survey companies that will pay you cash or gift cards to give them feedback on stores and restaurants you regularly enjoy. I utilized Market Force Survey and other companies to generate extra income. My experience with this company was great! I served as a mystery shopper at my selected restaurants, received a refund for the cost of my meal, and I got paid for my services. There was a four hour maximum requirement between surveys and I could do only three surveys per day. However, when I was short on cash, I would set up my mystery shopping time for breakfast, lunch and dinner. If you did not catch that, I got breakfast, lunch and dinner for free plus received a few extra dollars for each meal.

Utilizing your vehicle to generate cash is now in popular demand. However, dealing with the public in your personal space carries a risk. Make sure to do your research and understand the requirements, benefits, and risk factors.

Investing is one of the most favorable means to generate passive income. Be realistic with your investments. Know your limits and risks and seek an advisor. The higher the return usually means the higher the risk of losing your initial investment. Research the market, stocks, and bonds to see what the best fit is for you. You don't have to start investing with all your savings. You can start with what you can afford. There are several penny and nickel stocks you can invest in to get introduced to the market; as well as many over a thousand dollar investments available.

Some of the lower risk investments can be found at financial institutions locally or online. Warning: Before banking with financial institutions online make sure you do your due diligence to ensure they are legit and are covered by FDIC.

Earn small interest on your money through interest

bearing savings accounts and bank certificate deposits (CDs). Investing in savings bonds is a slow but risk-free way to generate cash. You can purchase a savings bond for half the face value, then cash the savings bond after 20 or 30 years, depending on the series, to double your investment. So if the savings bond is worth 50 dollars, you can purchase it for 25 dollars. The savings bond will generate interest yearly; however, not reach face value until the full maturity.

Have you ever thought about becoming a silent business partner? Research small businesses looking for investors. You can reap the profits of your initial investment without doing much. Of course, you want to do your due diligence and make sure it's the best opportunity and a risk you can accept. The business owner will manage all the daily operations, while you act as a silent partner and collect profits. You can also partner with family and friends you trust, then collectively purchase a franchise or investment property. Network to surround yourself with individuals who have success in these fields. Take online classes to learn more about the process.

The following are suggestions for additional ways to

generate income.

• Sign up for credit cards that have rewards like cash back, points, or mileage. Make sure you manage your credit cards productively.

• Sell professional photographs online. If you have a talent for capturing great photographs of scenery or other objects, there are websites such as Shutterstock you can earn cash from.

• Become a blogger by setting up your own website or purchasing an already popular abandoned blogger site. Buying an already established blog site will have a costly upfront cost, but if managed correctly you can earn back your investment plus generate extra income.

• Create a YouTube channel. Do your research to determine the demands and incorporate that into your channel. Creating videos is a rapidly growing business across America. Attaching Google AdSense to your videos will also generate income when your viewers click on the ads. There is a lot of general work that goes into setting up a successful YouTube channel but once it's complete it creates passive income.

• Create and host online courses. If you have a specialized skill, why not share it with the world and charge for it. There are so many courses you can offer such as the basic fundamentals of learning a new language, playing an instrument, designing a website design, or preparing taxes.

• You can write a book and produce multiple products from the book such as eBook, audio book, or workbook. It takes a lot of work to complete but once it's finished you create your audience platform.

• If you make jewelry, clothing or anything that is unique put in the time to increase your inventory. Then sell your products online or at social events.

There are so many resources available to create passive income. Take some time and research to see what other people are doing and try it. If it's not for you, try something else.

Bri Jones

# BUDGETING WITH A PURPOSE

*T*  *hrough wisdom a house is built, and by understanding it is established: and by knowledge the rooms shall be filled with all precious and pleasant riches* - Proverbs 24:3-4 (AKJV)

Budgeting is an fundamental factor of financial success. Good budget management practices are of great benefit to individuals and organizations with any range of income and expenses. The ideal goal is to have income exceed all expenses by sixty percent. However, that is not always the circumstances. A budget plan can be created in simple or detailed terms; this at the discretion of the individual or organization. Before beginning the budget process, recognize your goal and purpose for creating additional savings. Remember this can be anything you want it to be. Examples are discussed in the Setting Goals chapter.

To begin, identify your monthly income. This includes income you take home after taxes from work and any other income you generate on a monthly basis such as interest, dividends, and investments. Next, calculate all your current monthly expenses such as rent/mortgage, utilities, groceries, debt payments, transportation, entertainment, and so on. Now, break down and categorize each expense you accumulate monthly. These categories will be identified as essential, secondary needs, wants, and unnecessary wants. Essential needs are basic necessities that allow you to live your daily life including shelter, utilities, food, basic clothing, healthcare, transportation and taxes. Secondary needs are productive things that make life easier but not extravagant such as basic cell phone, laptop and internet. Wants are anything you do not need to survive but makes living enjoyable such as vacations, dining out, social entertainment, cable television, gym membership, non-basic clothes, and pets. Unnecessary wants are anything else you purchase just because it is available for purchase on impulse such as junk food, technology, or a new model cell phone.

**Homework:** Create four labels for the categories: Essentials, Secondary Needs, Wants, and Unnecessary Wants. These labels can be placed in separate shoeboxes, jars, or whatever small containers you have around your home. It is necessary to keep the categories separate. For one week (Sunday - Sunday) keep all receipts for every purchase you make, then place the receipts in the respective category's jar or shoebox. At the end of the week, calculate the total for each category and study your spending habits. This will give you the visual understanding of where your money is going. Identify areas where you can improve and decide what you are willing to go without temporarily or permanently to increase your savings.

During Week Two, avoid purchasing anything that is not essential. This means only purchase what you need to live your daily life for that week. If you have food in your refrigerator or freezer, utilize that food first before shopping for additional food. However, if grocery shopping is necessary, make a shopping list and collect coupons. Prepare all meals at home for lunch and dinner for the week. Avoid dining out. Show restraint! You can do it! At the end of the week collect all your receipts and place them separately from Week One in the respective categories. Total each category. Theoretically, there should be only one jar with receipts. If not, hopefully you see an improvement from the previous week. After totaling all the receipts for each category for Week Two, compare totals with Week One. Hopefully, you see a noticeable savings in Week Two. If not, don't get discouraged. This exercise was for you to identify your strengths and weaknesses in your weekly expenditures.

Now, let's create some new habits and sacrifices! What does sacrifice look like?

Sacrifice is the willingness to surrender something in exchange for something greater. Continuous reminders of the goals you want to accomplish make the sacrifices worth it. Take a moment and walk around your home. Look in your refrigerator, freezer, food pantry, cabinets, bedrooms, closets, bathrooms, basement, storage area or unit, and laundry room.

Let's start with your kitchen such as food pantry, refrigerator and freezer. How often do you throw away expired, freezer burnt or molded food from your kitchen? How often do you dine out, and then bring leftovers home only to throw them away a week later? How much money do you think you are really throwing away weekly or monthly? Every time you throw away food, you are throwing away money. This is a careless money mismanagement practice. Several years ago, I used to do a lot of bulk shopping once a month and subconsciously practiced that same cycle. I would have a long day at work; then I would pick up dinner for my son and me, while food wasted away in the kitchen. Sadly, I did this for years.

Unknowingly, my friends became my wake up call. I have several friends from different countries around the world and I always enjoy their sharing their culture with me. My friends collectively educated me on how they consider "grocery shopping" in their respective countries. In some countries, they had to go to the market daily to get only the food they needed for that day and possibly the next day. This was because they had limited refrigerator space, if any, and no freezer to preserve the food for several days or months. In addition, many countries have a limited amount of food available to eat, let alone to waste. Also, in these different cultures the portion of food they consumed in one meal was sometimes half the size of what Americans consume in one meal.

While growing up, I was made aware of the resources

we have that other countries did not. However, as an adult it was only upon hearing it from my friends that I developed a new mindset to eliminate waste.

It's about retraining your mindset. Evaluate your expenses and eliminate unnecessary waste.

Here is my challenge to you. Eat all the food you have in your home before you purchase any more groceries. Set one day during the week to dine out and stick to it. You can always change the day of the week. Just limit dining out to one day a week. Going forward, only purchase groceries that you know you will consume within that current week. Prepare your shopping list by identifying the meals you plan to make that week. Mentally visualize those meals and write your meal plan for the week and post it on your refrigerator. This will help your mental senses to accomplish the goal for that week. Collect and separate coupons that correspond with the shopping list. Once you have created your grocery list and have all your coupons together, select a day when you will go grocery shopping. You want to shop with a purpose.

**Rule of thumb:** Eat before going to the grocery store;

never go there hungry. Only go to the sections of the grocery store that apply to your shopping list. Do not browse. When selecting items on your list, compare prices to take advantage of the best savings. Use the cost per ounce to identify the savings and the needs for your household. Of course, some foods you can purchase in bulk because they have a greater shelf life and can be applied to several meals such as rice, grains, or dry beans. While waiting in the checkout lines read a magazine or check your email to avoid temptation of impulsive purchases by the register.

Now let's talk about a few other things you can consider to cut costs around the house to generate more savings and less waste.

| Unplug appliances not in use |
| Adjust thermostat by two degree increments |
| Use library for free entertainment |
| Use natural light |
| Wash clothes in cold water |
| Stop bad habits |
| Take quick quality showers |
| Stop living outside of your means |

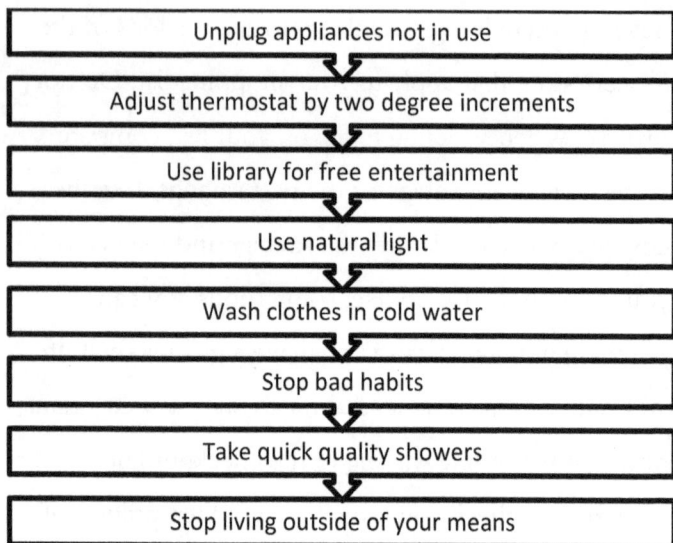

• Unplug appliances when not in use such as television, computer, microwave, and electronics. Even when items are plugged in but not turned on, they are absorbing power.

• Adjust thermostat by two degrees. This will prevent your heating or cooling unit from pulling so much power to get your home to the set temperature. Gradually adjusting the thermostat saves money and preserves your temperature unit. In addition, lower the thermostat when leaving home and at night. Keeping your thermostat at a minimum of 65 degrees in the winter will keep your pipes from freezing and keeping your thermostat at a maximum 75 degrees will keep moisture from building up in your pipes. You should also utilize blankets and socks in the winter to decrease the demand for turning the thermostat up too high.

• Use the library for free entertainment such as books, movies, and compact disks. The library usually keeps up with the latest movie releases on digital video disc (DVD). The library has access to pull items from surrounding libraries if they do not have what you are looking for in stock.

• Use natural light during the day to lower your electric expenses and turn off lights when they are not needed. If you walk out of a room, get in the habit of turning off the lights especially if you're not returning right away.

• Washing clothes in cold water will reduce your electric expenses. It takes energy for your water heater to keep the water hot or warm. Clothes will still get clean in cold water. Washing clothes in full loads will result in less water and energy being wasted.

• Stop bad habits such as smoking and drinking beer and liquor. These habits are not only costing you a lot of money now, but they could eventually cost you your health.

- Instead of going to expensive fancy coffee cafes, make your fresh cup at home. Invest in a reasonable coffee or latte machine so you can save yourself over $2,000 per year.

- Take only the necessary time needed to take a shower. Do not let the water run in excess before getting in the shower or even when washing dishes.

- Pay bills on time. You will save money by avoiding excessive late fees. This will also benefit your credit.

Review your budget regularly every 30 days. Make modifications to your budget plan when necessary. Always save money where you can. Once you get comfortable with your budget plan, set up your recurring bills to automatic bill pay and recurring automatic withdrawal to a separate savings account.

Bri Jones

# MAINTAIN CREDIT STABILITY

*T*he rich rules over the poor, and the borrower becomes the lender's slave - Proverbs 22:7 (NASB)

Establishing and maintaining good credit is a challenge for many people. Oftentimes, we were never informed about what having good credit really means and how it can affect our lives. In most situations, having no credit is considered just as dreadful as having bad credit. Your credit report is not only viewed by creditors in making decisions to approve the purchase of a vehicle or house, it is also used to determine the interest rate you will pay on your respective purchases. Depending on your credit report, you could pay low or high interest rates on your respective purchases. High interest rates could result in paying three times the amount of the original cost of your purchase. Your credit report could affect your career. Many employers are reviewing credit reports before hiring qualified candidates.

TransUnion, Equifax and Experian are the three major credit reporting bureaus that provide a report on your credit. These three major credit reporting bureaus contribute to the FICO (credit) Scores ranging from 300-850. You are entitled to receive a free annual credit report per federal law from each of the major credit reporting bureaus at annualcreditreport.com. It is critical to examine your credit report annually. There could be erroneous reports affecting your FICO Score such as outstanding payments that were paid, defaulted loans that were paid off, outdated information, or fraud. These inaccuracies can be corrected. Contact the credit bureaus that are reporting the inaccurate information via telephone and request for them to rectify the mistakes (TransUnion 800-916-8800, Equifax 866-349-5191 and Experian 888-397-3742). Follow up by sending a letter reiterating the same request as you made over the telephone and notifying the three credit reporting bureaus of the anticipated changes.

 Bad credit and excessive debt are stressful and can affect your health. It is valuable to understand what affects your credit score. Payment history determines 35 percent of your credit score. When creditors examine your credit report, they are looking to see if you are a high risk according to your payment patterns. Creditors base your approval and interest rate on the likelihood of your paying back the money you are requesting to borrow. If creditors approve you for a loan but you are still a high risk, then the creditor will assign a higher interest rate. When you have a high interest rate, you can pay up to triple the original amount of the loan once it meets maturity. Consider this, if your loan is pass due or charged off the creditors will charge you higher interest rates on your next loan. This means the creditors will collect more money from you through excessive fees and other add-ons because you're will be considered a high risk. Don't give creditors free money!

Debt-to-income (DTI) ratio is the total debt cost per month divided by your monthly income. The rule is that your debt-to-income ratio should never exceed 36 percent. Debt-to-income ratio includes all expenses appearing on your credit report, but do not include utilities, insurance, groceries or other similar expenses. If your debt-to-income ratio is greater than 36 percent then this will affect the creditor's decision on future approvals and the interest rate given to you.

Multiple inquiries from vehicle, mortgage, or student loan lenders within a short period of time does not usually affect your credit score directly. However, applying for several credit cards and generating multiple inquiries within a short period of time can cause you to be considered a high risk when reviewed by creditors. Public records such as bankruptcies, judgments, and collection items may lower your credit score. Opening multiple new accounts in a short period of time may have a negative impact on your credit score. Also, having numerous open accounts can have a harmful affect to your credit score. However, having a long credit history can have a positive impact on your credit score if managed correctly.

Establishing credit can sometimes be just as difficult as rebuilding your credit. Oftentimes, some of the same practices apply to both. Most financial institutions have products and programs that focus on establishing and rebuilding credit. Depending on your financial institution (traditional bank or credit union), there is a product called secured credit card. You have to apply for the secured credit card the same way you would for a regular credit card and wait for an approval. One common version of the secured credit card is similar to a prepaid card. The initial cash is withdrawn from your account and applied to the credit card and that represents your credit limit. However, there is still an interest rate fee that applies to the outstanding balance. Another common version of the secured credit card is half the credit limit is provided by the consumer and the other half is loaned by the financial institution.

Become a co-signer or authorized user on a responsible family or friend's credit card or loan. Make sure this person values a good credit score status. You don't need to have access to the family or friend's credit card or loan. This technique is only for you to benefit from their good financial habits.

Make sure you pay all your bills on time such as rent, utilities, and especially student loans. Even though some rental properties and utilities do not regularly report to the credit bureaus when you are on time, remember they definitely will if you're late. It's better to request to put your student loans in forbearance than to be late. Being late on student loans will have a negative impact on your credit score.

When establishing or rebuilding your credit, it is significant to pay off the credit balance in three month increments. A great practice is if you don't have the cash to pay for the item, don't purchase it. Yes, you can use your credit card to establish or maintain your credit score, but if you don't have the money in the bank to pay off the credit card within three months, then you should reconsider purchasing the product. You want your credit history to demonstrate you can manage your debt successfully. An example of a good practice is if you charge one hundred dollars in January; when you receive the credit card statement due February 18th pay 70 dollars for this statement and for the follow billing cycles pay 15 dollars in March and the remaining balance in April. Most credit card companies report to the credit bureaus for 60 or 90 day cycles. However, there are a few credit card companies that report monthly to the credit bureaus. You should never charge more than 33 percent of your credit limit. For example, if you have a credit limit of 1,000 dollars, do not charge over 330 dollars. You don't want your credit report to reflect that you are depending on credit to survive.

A common mistake as a consumer is opening multiple

new credit or debt accounts, instead you should contact the creditor and request an increase in your credit limit. This will have a positive effect on your credit report. You can also request a credit limit increase when you exceed 33 percent to avoid the negative impact on your credit report.

To reach the ultimate goal of being debt free and having a great credit score takes discipline, sacrifice, time and most of all a plan. It is possible! Fixing your credit has more processes than establishing your credit. If paying your bills on time has not been a habit, then this should be something you focus on. Set your bills up as auto pay and add them to your mobile phone calendar as a reminder.

List all your debt from smallest to largest balance. Since we discussed in the previous chapter how to create passive income and implementing a budget plan, this additional savings will be helpful in paying off your debt. There are a few approaches you can attempt to eliminate your credit card balance evaluate which one fits your situation.

∞    Once you list all your debt, contact your high

balance creditors to negotiate a payoff settlement. Follow the requirement of the creditor for the new approved payoff settlement. If you don't have the cash available to pay off the debt, consolidate the new payoff settlement amounts to a credit card that is offering a zero percent interest rate and zero transfer fees. Credit card companies often offer zero percent interest rate balance transfers for twelve months. Make sure you read the fine print and understand what the interest rate and fees will be once the zero percent interest rate special ends. Try to avoid credit cards that require an annual fee. When the 12 month zero percent interest rate special is over, you will be charged an increase interest rate on the whole balance that remains on that credit card. The goal is to pay down or pay off the principal balance before the 12 month zero percent interest rate expires. This is a great opportunity to consolidate all your credit cards and save money on accumulated interest fees you would have been charged on the individual credit cards. You should consider paying the additional money you would have been charged in interest fees from the individual credit cards toward the balance of the consolidated credit card. Structure a strict budget during the twelve months in an effort to pay off the complete balance of the consolidated credit card.

∞ Start focusing on paying off your smallest balance first; then, work your way up to paying off the largest balance. To do this, maintain your minimum balance payments for all your debt except your smallest debt balance. Remember the goal is to pay off the smallest debt to the largest debt in that order. For example, you have five credit cards with a credit balance of $500; $1,000; $2,500; $5,000; and $10,000. For this example, assume your minimum payment due for each card is $30. For each payment cycle your will pay a total of $120 ($30 payments for each credit cards except the $500 balance). For the $500 credit balance you will pay as much as you can in excess of the minimum $30 requirement. Once the $500 credit card is paid off, then apply the same step to the $1,000 balance; but now apply the additional payment you would have paid on the $500 balance to the $1,000 payment. Once you're ready to focus on the payoff of the high credit balances, contact the creditor to negotiate a settlement balance with a payment plan. Continue to repeat these steps until all debt is paid off.

Once you pay off your credit card, do not close the card. Simply cut up the card so you won't be tempted to use it. Closing a credit card after you pay it off may have a negative effect on your credit score. Closing your credit card demonstrates to your creditors that you cannot handle or manage having excess credit available.

Bri Jones

# REWARDING YOURSELF

*W*ithout counsel, plans are frustrated, but with many counselors they will succeed." -Proverbs 15:22 (NASB)

Sometimes we get so focused on achieving our goal that we forget to enjoy the journey on the way. Having a consistent reward system is an essential habit to practice when achieving a goal. It is just as significant to reward yourself when reaching small milestones as it is to achieving your final goal. There are many reasons why it is imperative to celebrate your success such as; motivation to work harder, staying on track, feeling achievement, and building confidence. Depending on the goal you set, dedication and sacrifices can be challenging. Applying positive reinforcement when completing small goals generates momentum to the brain. This causes you to react more effortlessly in the direction of completing the ultimate goal more naturally.

For a more challenging goal, decide in advance the

reward for achieving your goal as additional encouragement. Not all reward milestones should be equally distributed. Select rewards that are encouraging to you for your success. A reward does not need to be extravagant, but the reward should match the goal. Make the reward visible. Place a picture of the reward in a location that you will see daily without effort. This is a constant reminder of what you're looking forward to when you achieve your goal.

It is significant to make sure your reward is affordable once you achieve your goal. The worst thing you can do to yourself is set your hopes up for disappointment especially after working so hard to achieve your goal. Never contradict your goal with rewards that defeat the purpose of the goal. Find your motivator. Do something meaningful and affordable.

Rewarding yourself for small goals or milestones doesn't have to be materialistic. Congratulating yourself out loud (when no one else is around), patting yourself on the back, displaying a proud smile, doing a happy dance, or yelling in excitement are just a few of the Free! Reward systems that you can implement as routine habits for successfully completing a goal on a budget.

Additional reward systems to consider are; spa day, lazy day, weekend getaway, hotel getaway, going out with friends, buying a new outfit, sleeping in, volunteering, or donating to charity.

Write down your goal and the required steps to achieve the goal. Determine how you want to measure your progress and clarify that you're on track and going in the right direction to achieve your goal. Remember; never contradict your goals with your reward system. If your goal is to save money, don't reward yourself with an extravagant gift. Instead, do something inexpensive or Free! Continue to build your confidence and momentum to take on more challenging goals to lead to a more successful you.

> *"Success is liking yourself,*
>
> *liking what you do,*
>
> *and liking how you do it."*
>
> *— Maya Angelou*